AF316780

I Know I Am Better
than What
I Was Told...

*A Remarkable Way to Break What Holds You
from Creating the Life You Want*

Gil Evans

Gil Evans Soul Journey
7009 Hill Avenue
Holland, OH 43528
www.gilevans.net

ISBN: 979-8-3302-3873-6

First published by AuthorHouse: 2018.
Second edition by Gil Evans: 2024.

I know I am Better than What I was told…
A Remarkable Way to Break what Holds You from Creating the Life You Want.

Written by Gil Evans.

www.gilevans.net

This book was created to help you break through those things that hold you back.

The things in life that happen to us,
the people who try to control our
feelings and things.

This book is a dedication to my beautiful wife, Jennifer Evans, who had awakened the love in me, my mentors throughout my life; Reid Harrington, for my awakening as a leader, my detention teacher who taught me my value; Mr. Ronald Van Dresen, and my mother Mary Emerita Rodriguez, R.I.H., who taught me what it truly means to serve others.

TABLE OF CONTENTS

INTRODUCTION

I decided to write this book as it tells a lot about how I was able to overcome some of the adversities in my life. I use a lot of the content when I coach others.

Growing up was a challenging time for me and my siblings. We were poor, in a cult, and were mentally and physically abused because of our parents' cult beliefs. This made life hard as I always knew there had to be better. I left home at the age of 13 to find the truth for me, and this book is my journey.

I made many mistakes during my voyage to find out who I was and what was true. I built three multi-million-dollar companies from nothing. I made a lot of money and lost a lot.

What I realized is that my journey in life was the pursuit of happiness. The money, and things, meant nothing without being grateful for what I have and happy with who I have become. The pillars of success, health, wealth, and happiness are false. True wealth is living happily and healthily. I found out that without these two pillars, wealth or success means nothing. Money and things don't equate to a successful life.

It is sad that to this day, some of my siblings hold these experiences in them, which kept them from reaching their full potential. I sure hope they have their awakening someday.

The idea, I grew up in poverty, broke free from the clutches of a Cult and abusive homelife, had the lowest self-esteem, was dyslexic, and became homeless to find my true self. With determination and belief, there was better, I fought through tough times, built my healthy self-image and knowledge, and became a successful entrepreneur, and leader.

After all these years of being a poor reader, I have published numerous articles focusing on self-improvement and leadership principles. I have coached hundreds of people and helped thousands move on a path of better lives and careers.

I hope you find value in this book as I did live it.

I knew I was better than I was told…

Gil Evans

CHAPTER 1

DESIRE

We all have this inner desire to create a life of fulfillment.

Sadly, most do not realize we all have this burning within us.

Desire to me means a burning to be, have, or hunger for something better than where we are. Our desires push us to do more so we can bring to life the things we see ourselves wanting.

Desire should never be mistaken for wishing. Wishing we had a better life, wishing we were better than what we were. Wishes will not come true unless we truly desire the things in life we want.

This chapter is my development of desiring to obtain a better life than I had.

Growing up, my experiences were challenging as a child. We were very poor, and to make it worse, we were in a cult.

My mother's family was from Mexico and their beliefs for a normal lifestyle was the life of a migrant worker. During our summers, we would work in fields picking strawberries, pickles, or hoeing row after row of crops.

I remember arriving at the farms not happy as a child. All I wanted to do was play during the summers. Unfortunately, we had to work 14-hour days in the heat.

If we arrived early in the season to the farms, we would be able to live in small shacks about 12 ft. by 24 ft. long. They had a kitchen/living room and one bedroom. If they were taken, you had the choice of living in your car or sleeping in barns. I always thought we weren't that lucky as my aunt would pick the concrete pads to sleep on where the farmers stored their tractors.

I thought that the bales of hay that some families were sleeping on would have been more comfortable; however, she knew that that stuff was itchy.

Photo taken by Gil Evans. Migrant camp in Ohio

We would get up before the sun showed its head, to start working. We would work all day long, rarely taking a break. We would finally be able to rest once the farmer called it quits when the sun went down.

We worked hard. I was not sure if the heat was the worst or the tiny pickers on pickles that stuck in your skin. Wearing gloves was no good as they slowed your ability to pick efficiently. We did what we were told and had to pick a certain number of baskets every day or get beat. I think I liked getting beat as I rarely made my quota.

There were no bathrooms in the fields, only cornfields. I will not go there, but you can guess where everyone did his or her business. Today I remember sharing water out of a bucket with a ladle, sharing this with so many people. Today it is somewhat disgusting thinking about it. Back then, it was part of life. I did not experience anything better, but I knew there was better.

One day, my mom and I went to the farmer's

house to pick up our weekly check. This house is massive! I was so amazed.

I asked my mother, "Mom, why do some people have homes like this, and we have nothing"? She said in her Spanglish way; "Mijo (my son), some people are born rich, and we were born to serve others". Man, I thought, this is not true, I am not a slave. I knew there had to be more than this. I was eight years old, and I knew I was better than that. I would never be anyone's slave. I liked working, but no way would I do this for the rest of my life!

My mother wasn't the only one teaching us that the rich are privileged in ways we weren't. It was a common lesson in our lives, but I could not believe this was true. Was it? I would never tell my mother she was wrong. I loved her and would not want to hurt her, not to mention you never doubt a Mexican mother or you will be hit.

Religious and social beliefs were the foundation of my family. My parents were in a cult where its beliefs were physically and mentally beaten into you. You showed respect no matter what. The cult had a workbook on how to get respect and steps on how to control your family through various punishing techniques—specifically written for control of children and wives.

My father worked two or three jobs and I remember going home on the weekends and crying to him to allow us to stay home. That was not an option.

There were five siblings at the time. I was just eight years old. We weren't allowed to be children. We had to obey my father or not just one of us would get beat, but all of us. He would continue beating us until we all quieted down. This was hard as we were getting beaten with his belt all over except for our faces. I remember the welts on us afterward. I also remember my mother coating us with rubbing alcohol. This was so painful, but I believe she felt this would help cleanse and heal our wounds.

We were children, but we were robbed of all childhood innocence and wonder.

The cult did not believe in the holidays. During times like Christmas and Easter, outside family members would bring us Easter candy, or Christmas gifts. They would have Easter egg hunts in the yard, and we reluctantly followed in on the excitement.

I remember my uncles would bring us toys for Christmas. For a small amount of time, we could be like regular kids, even though we knew it was evil to play with these toys, we couldn't stop the temptation and joy of being a child. As soon as the family left, my father would destroy the toys and then the belt came off.

None of this made sense even after all these years. Since we were young, ages five through nine, it was always impossible to comprehend why that was our life. It always felt like we did something wrong.

As siblings experiencing the same horrors, we were determined to help comfort each other to stop the screaming from the lashes. It is amazing what love for each other does to kill pain and fear. Eventually, it goes away and later in my life, I realized that the past pain could kill your love and spirit if you let it.

This was the first time I realized my true desire. We were all in pain and no matter what happened; we had the desire to help each other get through this. Even through pain, we had to stay determined to reach our only goal. At that moment, it was comforting each other to quiet down.

It is hard to write about this as it does bring back that deep burning gut feeling you get before something bad is going to happen.

That burning in your stomach where you want to lose your bladder and die.

As I got a little older, I remembered what my mom said about us being put on this earth to serve others. This idea didn't stick with me. I knew I was better than that and was determined to prove it.

My desire to become better than what I was told was sewn deep into me.

Desire to change, do better, grow, and become something awakens our spirit and strengthens us.

Sometimes pain creates this desire, as we want to escape it.

THE DESIRE TO BE MORE

The cult had different groups within. It had its own Boy Scout troop, singles club, choir, acting for plays, and others. This was my third experience with desire. I remember I always liked the idea of being the popular or famous one, the singer, or the funny person in school. I pushed and did whatever I could, so I would stand out in the crowd. I had the desire for attention from others.

I involved myself in as much as possible to be the center of attention. In choir, would sing louder than everyone else. I did whatever was possible for the limelight and to stick out of the crowd.

I remember the day I went from Cub Scout to Boy Scout. We were on a stage and this one teenager, Dwight, was standing at the end of the stage, becoming an Eagle Scout. I was mesmerized by all the cool badges and the prestige he had. At that moment, I said to myself, **"In one year, I will be standing up here and I will be an Eagle Scout."** That day my desire grew to that one goal, becoming an Eagle Scout.

I pushed for every badge I could get. I had so many badges; I filled my sash and sleeves. I had badges in my pocket. If there were a record for merit badges earned in one year, I would have had that record. I went through that merit badge book taking anything, even farm records.

The year came to an end and I did it! I had all the necessary accomplishments and more to be an Eagle Scout. I went to my scout leader to see when I could become an Eagle Scout.

Mr. D. said, **"No! You're not old enough to be one."** I was devastated.

I remember feeling like how Ralphie felt when in A Christmas Story his teacher told him, **"You'll shoot your eye out."** I went to my father crying and told him what happened. He said the same. So, what did I do? I QUIT! I was done! I quit on my dream and the thing I desired all that past year.

My desire fizzled that moment. I was still in the scouts because I was not allowed to leave. My desire to be more than I was disappeared. The cult used groups like the scouts as a controlling method of keeping you focused on staying true to the cult.

As we got older, the cult had a camp in Orr, Minnesota where teens would go for summer. Fun in the sun, camping, water sports, a fun-filled summer, or so we were told. It was a camp set up to brainwash teens to stay in the cult. The cult believed that as we become teenagers or young adults, we become more attuned to the world, so they created methods of keeping your focus on their beliefs. This was done through classes, regular beatings and mental abuse of the young adults.

I recently talked to an older friend that attended one of the camps. He told me he remembered the beatings more than the fun.

Eventually, I had numerous discussions with people who were teens in the cult. It was so amazing the pain they still live with because of the cult that they have been out of for over 40 years. Their lives and spirits were destroyed.

The most amazing thing that happened was the day we all talked. It was the day they started living again. Their awakening and desire to live a fulfilled life.

Throughout my learning, I have always had the

strength of desire to make it. When I put my mind to something, I put it all in to become successful.

> *What we hold in our mind, burns in our hearts and will either awaken or destroy our spirit.*

I held this pain in my heart and spirit for years. Although I may have seemed OK on the outside, I was lost. I was dying from the inside out. There wasn't anything that could make me happy. I was so jealous of others, and as a child, I was a bully. A bully to people who had more than me and a bully to others who were committed to their religion. I don't tell many about this, however, I was bad. In my heart, I knew my behavior was wrong, but I did not realize it all stemmed from the emptiness within. I was no longer certain if was real or not.

Alcohol became a friend at an early age. It helped me forget the pain and while I was inebriated, I was happy. I felt I was funny and could talk to people.

It was amazing. I was suddenly having fun and not caring about all the people I had been terrible towards. Self-centered, didn't care if I hurt them. It was all about me and my feelings. My rewards and my success.

> *The desire to prove people wrong can harm your spirit.*

My life was surrounded by one mistake after another. All my time was spent trying to prove I was more than I was told, trying to prove to the world that

I was important, and underneath it all, trying to prove to my mother that she was wrong. I was not put on this earth to serve others.

In a surprisingly positive twist in our lives, my mother finally left my father. It was a change that needed to happen, so she could break away from the cult.

This was my shot. My mother left home and needed somewhere to live. I told her to find a home and I would buy it for her. At a very young age, I was able to buy my mother a home.

She found the ugliest house with three acres of land. I was shocked, and asked her, **"Mom, is this what you want?"** She said, **"Yes, it is close to my friends and stores".** So, we bought it.

Mom lived there for five years then moved to help her sister in San Antonio, Texas.

When she returned to Ohio, she moved into low-income housing instead of the house I bought for her. I didn't understand. The house was only a quarter mile from the projects she moved into. I was confused and upset.

It took a while for me to understand that my mother needed to be surrounded by others she could help.

I had an issue with the house and was going to dump it. My wife and I came to town with the intention of remodeling and selling it. My wife and I had a disagreement while looking at the home. We went to different sides of the house to get away from each other and think. 20 minutes later, we both met halfway. We had fallen in love with the property.

We moved in and to this day, we still live in the

house. After too long, I realized the lesson she had tried to teach me: we live to serve/help others.

THE YEAR MY MOTHER DIED

Years ago, I made a great income. I worked hard to create a beautiful home from the house that was once my mother's. Our family would have their annual reunions in the backyard, and I always offered the house to my mother who organized everything.

We had plenty of space for cars, AC, a pool, and more yard for fun. I even offered to pay for all the food and beverages. Year after year to my family, I was turned down. My mother's words, **"No, we already have the park reserved."**

I always got upset and only went once to the reunion, as I was insulted that they wouldn't have it at my home.

When my mother was on her deathbed, I lay next to her and asked her, **"Mom, did I do something wrong that you didn't like me or my family?"** She looked at me in confusion as I explained about the offers, I had given, and the fact she never came over. I rarely came over to see her either. She looked at me and said, **"Mijo, oh I love you. You just never needed anything"**. This still echoes in my head.

All those years I tried to prove my mother wrong, that we weren't put on this earth to serve others. However, she was right. What she meant was true. Some were born rich, to her this meant they were self-serving, and cared only for themselves, not about others.

Others were born to serve, which meant helping

others get what they want.

My family kept their distance, and at work, it was different. My desire to help others get what they wanted out of life became my passion. This was rewarding, even though I was a stubborn ass while proving to myself I was better than I was told. I was a natural at helping others, and I was able serve to others like she taught me. I found my true desire.

> *If you desire success and a life of purpose, find a way to serve the masses. Both will come.*

Today, I have the desire to do what makes me happy. My life is focused on happiness. If it doesn't bring happiness to me, I don't do it.

My desire to help others get what they want out of life is the most rewarding thing I do.

I now realize that my mother choosing that once dilapidated home was not for her, it was her desire to help me become a better person. Her desire to help me appreciate life.

One thing I learned is we should be cautious about how many things we work on. Mistaking "want" for true desire can keep us from enjoying life. Especially when it comes to appreciation and happiness for what we have and who we have become. Having the desire to work on many things at once may hinder us from accomplishing anything and the desire soon fizzles out.

Desire can lose its steam of distractions and failures. We must keep pushing forward as we work towards what we want. Life and people will test you. You must stay focused and stay determined to reach the things you desire.

Work through the task till the end. Don't lose focus and never let anyone block your desire for what you want. Work your plan and stay the course.

Today my desire and light burn bright helping others get the most out of life and my continual pursuit of happiness.

> *Desire is the burning thing you believe in.*
> *We desire the feeling of importance of being somebody,*
> *the desire to love, and the desire to be loved.*

Simply our desire is the feeling to be needed.

CHAPTER 2

FAITH

Faith has many meanings faith is a necessity to create your life.

Faith has many meanings. Faith can be a spiritual sense of a higher spirit or god, and there's also a form of faith in oneself. You believe you can accomplish or create something in life when you have confidence in yourself. You put faith in others or the world to do things right.

During my childhood, my parents were involved in a large cult. This faith, like so many other cults, was started by one person's interpretation of the bible. As it developed, so did the founder's ideas for his new faith. His faith became an obsession and no other religion was right. Anyone who was outside his religious beliefs was part of the satanic world. Every holiday known to man, created by man, had reasons for why they were created to follow false gods.

The cult's obsession was so strong it created ways to brainwash and control its followers to believe that anything outside of this was evil. Violating this faith would result in the end of life and lead to an afterlife full of an eternal lake of fire where you would burn for eternity. At the age of 6, I was told numerous times that this was where I would end up and I truly believed I was going to burn forever. With my child's imagination, I could visualize the torturous afterlife I was reminded of time and time again.

Our lives were centered around following the orders of the cult. Every punishment, every beating, was **"for our own good."** We were beaten for any reason that was deemed not right by the church's standard. When people outside of the church would come to visit, playing seemed OK when they were there. Or, so we thought.

We were young children. I remember being locked up in a dark closet at night. My family would tell me that they were heading for the promised land, and I was locked in there for the devil to come and get me to take me to this lake of fire. I could hear my family walk away and hear the door shut.

This was cruel punishment, but it was my father's way of building our faith in the church through fear.

This type of mental and physical abuse showed the belief in me on the outside but on the inside, it created doubt of what was true. I was confused and lost.

At the age of 13, I left home to search for answers. I knew there was better, and I was going to find it. I was determined to find out who I was. Life being brainwashed doesn't leave you as you leave the environment, it strengthens. Not knowing what is right and what is wrong creates doubt in your decisions, and you lose trust in your actions and everyone around you. You lose all faith.

As an adult, I remember holidays with my family where they had to walk on eggshells around me because I would suddenly become hateful and distrust would set in. I didn't understand why. It wasn't intentional, it just happened. My children were from my wife's previous marriage, and she was catholic. So, Easter, Christmas, and Halloween were part of their culture. I had to find ways to heal from the clutches of my father's abuse and the cult. I needed to redefine these holidays differently, so I could either join in and enjoy this time with my family, or just accept them, step aside, and allow my family to enjoy their traditions. I wanted in and couldn't figure it out.

> *To be able to heal, we must believe in ourselves and the actions we take.*

Christmas seemed to be that time of year when, for a short amount of time, families got together and forgot all the bickering and just enjoyed each other's company.

This kindness and loving time intrigued me, so I decided it best to view Christmas as not a sinful holiday time, but as a loving time.

Once I did this, the holidays started becoming much more acceptable for me.

I once spoke to a group about changing my mental outlook, and a few people actually got upset that I took **"Christ out of Christmas."** My explanation for why wasn't acceptable to them. It wasn't about them and their beliefs, it was about mine and how I coped with this fight inside of me. This fight for truth allows me to be with my family enjoying these special times of year.

> *Sometimes we need to restructure what and how we think, to accept the things that create discomfort for ourselves.*

> *Building faith in a different way.*

Faith has another definition outside of the religious world. It is the belief in you and your actions and the confidence in your abilities or actions.

Your faith is the belief that you can do anything in life if you set your mind to do it. George Michaels' lyrics, "You got to have Faith, fuh, faith fuh faith" are so true. You must have faith for the good in the world, and in you.

When you decide on what you want in life, your faith that it will happen is most important. When you push hard to get through tough times, it's your faith in your pursuit that pushes you confidently through it.

As we realize our successes in life, it builds our faith. Faith is confidence. The belief is that we will get through tough times and the goals we set for ourselves.

When we fail time after time, it takes a little out of us sometimes, weakening our faith in our abilities, and losing our confidence in making simple decisions. We become afraid of making a move to correct things and give up. We lose faith in the world and ourselves.

Faith is our light that shines inside. As we lose our faith or confidence, our light dims. The wonderful thing is that it only takes little wines to brighten this light and build our faith.

THE BEST WAY IS TO DO TWO SIMPLE EXERCISES

Take an inventory of your accomplishments.

Start looking for those tiny accomplishments you have and quit focusing on your losses.

The more you accomplish the more your belief in yourself increases.

I always inventory my life, where I was at different times and even to the present day. I knew I was better than before. My faith in myself and my future is high. Those downturns are always temporary, and I always come out of them even stronger.

Not too long ago, I had an issue with a boss that hurt our whole team. They saw the issue arising and instead of working through it with the team, they bailed and left. We followed the lead of this person and because of this, our whole team was reprimanded. I was upset, and even though it was based on us following our boss's decisions, I felt disappointed, and let down, and for a moment, I lost faith in my company for their stance. I then took an inventory of my past wins, and this thing was defeating me for no reason.

It made me, and others, look bad in our new boss's eyes. I knew I was better than this as I have always performed well above average. I began to rebuild the view of me, coached others to do the same, and we all came back on top.

A huge win is not necessary to build faith in yourself, only a few small wins start the process.

When we have difficult situations in our lives, they block us from realizing we can get through this stuff. It chokes us keeping us from seeing the answers to release these issues.

When we were young, most of us had people play peek-a-boo with us. Sometimes we kept our eyes completely covered with your hands and fingers, sometimes we left spaces in our hands enabling us to see a little.

Photo by, Heather Moses, of her beautiful daughter, Maddy Moses

The more situations that we hold in ourselves are like peek-a-boo. Every time we put a finger in front of our eyes, eventually covering both our eyes, we lose complete sight of what is happening around us. This is how our mind works.

Like the fingers covering our eyes, blocking our vision, each issue we have blocked out our sight which keeps us from seeing the answers that are in front of us.

We need to break away from this thing that blinds us from moving on. Like spreading our fingers that are covering our eyes, one at a time, so we can start building clarity, regaining our sight to find answers to the things that hold us prisoner to our thoughts.

So, as you do the next exercise, it will enable you to pull back one finger at a time, or depending on how big the situation is, it will give you just enough sight for you to start resolving your issue.

The more you use this exercise the more clarity, and strength you will get. You will see yourself breaking through anything.

CUT THE CORD

There are times when no matter what we do, we can't seem to drop the situation(s) bugging us and we think about it all day long.

We think about it all day and when we go to bed, we either cannot sleep, or we dream about it. We beat ourselves up or go into a state of depression.

Cutting the cord is an old exercise to create a visualization to move away from the situation. It still may be there, but it is out of our minds, so we can create clarity and move on.

In a quiet room, stand up straight. Picture yourself as a Samurai warrior with your Samurai sword drawn (a sign of power). Visualize a HUGE gold frame containing the person who is the issue or a symbolic image of the difficult situation. In the frame can be an invoice or payment due, someone annoying at work, someone controlling you or making you feel inferior, court documents, tax bills, etc.

Now, imagine a cord connected from your belly button to the frame.

Next, with your hands, as if you had this Samaria Sword, slice the cord while saying, **"Cut the cord."** Draw the sword up, again say, "cut the cord", and swing again while you say it. On the third swipe, repeating the words, picture you are cutting through this umbilical cord, severing the cord, and releasing the situation from your body.

Picture it is floating away from you. You've broken free from what drains you. This may take a few times to learn and visualize while you are physically doing the motions during this exercise.

As you become more aware and stronger with this, you will be able to swipe your hand in front of you three times while saying the words, "cut the cord" without the visualization.

This works so great; I taught many people this practice. It worked so well. My wife taught her team as well and they used it during tough situations at work making them pull out of their issues and move on.

So, when you have heard someone use the expression, **"cut the cord,"** you know why. They may not know the exercise but have heard the words.

> *To get clarity when times are tough, remember to.*
> *Cut the cord.*

CHAPTER 3

APPRECIATION

To change our way of thinking, we must appreciate the small things life has to give us.

During my earlier years, I founded numerous multi-million-dollar companies, and I made a lot of money, but I was never happy. I was successful, and I had developed record-breaking skills in business. I won culinary awards and helped inspire many people to better their lives, but still, I could not find life satisfaction. I was empty inside.

Something was always missing. I could not find happiness in my accomplishments. I started acting out and treating people unfairly, especially my friends and my family. I do not know how my wife put up with it for so many years.

I always had this emptiness in me, and I became desperate to find happiness through satisfaction in everything I did which caused me to be hypercritical of others.

I always wanted more. That is when I discovered that drinking would calm this part of me. The sedative state helped me cope with the emptiness.

After years of consuming so much alcohol, I did not realize it was killing me. On the outside, I seemed okay, but on the inside, I felt broken. One day my body decided to believe my mind and started to shut down.

I found myself getting sick repeatedly, and I finally woke up, got out of bed, and drove myself to the hospital. I was ill and I knew something was wrong. I remember when I checked into the emergency, I did not tell my wife as it was about 3:00 A.M. and she had to be at work at 6:00 A.M.

They admitted me and placed me in a room that seemed huge and dark. After what seemed to be an eternity, the doctor came in the room, sat next to me, and solemnly said, **"We got your results back and your test shows you had a heart attack."** I was scared, devastated, and alone.

I called my wife at work and, of course, she was upset and scared. Thinking back on it now, I should have let her know, but I had been in and out of the hospital for various things for about a month previous and I did not want to bother her.

That week I spent in the hospital was my new awakening. I had time to reflect on my life and what brought me to this point. The next day, they realized it was not a heart attack, but an inner infection that was causing my organs to shut down. My kidney had stones imbedded inside the walls and it was only the beginning. My liver and other organ functions declined more and more.

Sometimes, it takes a punch in the face to wake our spirit.

MY TRUE AWAKENING

The urologist came into my room, and we talked about the concern she had with my fatty liver. She asked if I drank. I drank every day, and I drank a lot. I refrained from drinking at work, but when I got home, I drank as if it was Kool-Aid.

I lied to the doctor and said I consumed half of what I did, which was more than the average person was. She was stunned and said I needed to stop.

After she left, I was ashamed of the lie. I called her back in to tell her the truth. This person was trying to save my life and I lied because of my embarrassment.

I remember my wife's eyes and face of shock when I told the doctor my truth. This truth was the start of a new person, my awakening. I was finished lying to others but done with lying to myself. This thing was sedating me enough that it masked the pain and depressed state I created. I had no control of my life, and this needed to stop, as it was not me.

That week, the more I reflected, the more I started to see everything I had been blind to while drinking. It humbled me.

One of my last days in the hospital, I remember staring out of the window, and I asked myself, **"What brought me to this point in life?"** Whatever it was, I never wanted to be in this situation again.

That day I made a commitment to myself: I would change everything bad in my life, especially drinking, and would build life, a better life. I started to appreciate the new beginning I was offered. There is nothing that I will do that could lead me back to that place I was before. I would do whatever was needed to become a healthier and better person.

I believe that the higher power/God said, **"Hey, it's time to wake up. You are going the wrong way, and you have work to do."**

The emptiness started to subside. Suddenly, everything mattered-- my wife, my children, my friends, and mostly, the value of my life.

I started looking for the good in my experiences and appreciating the tiniest moments that presented themselves to me. This new appreciation for life created a new version of me.

My eyes were finally open to the beauty in the world instead of focusing on the darkness of my past. I have a new vision now. A new appreciation for everything around me. This new appreciation and awakening of my spirit opened a new dimension of visualization of the world around me. Some believe in that vision; some think I am crazy.

When you appreciate the tiny things, your vision becomes enhanced. There are amazing lights and energies we can see when our hearts are open to them.

The past few years' life has been enlightening and inspiring. I love this new sight! I can see the good in people. The greatest thing is, I can see the good in me.

My biggest lesson was that by appreciating everything in life, all of the small things, I could change and be better.

> *To be able to live, we must believe in ourselves, see the good in everything, and appreciate where we are at this moment, as we created us, that we are amazing spirits in this world. We are only here for a short amount of time.*

Appreciate the people in your life, friends, family, and co-workers. Look for the good in them and only see this. We concentrate on the tiny negative things that bother us about someone, never appreciating the good even if it is small but good.

Remember, appreciating the tiny stuff eventually builds to huge, inspiring, and awakening our emotional senses. Today, I am floored away at the tiniest things in life. My heart still stops in a fraction of a second when I see my wife. I am so appreciative of her and the love she has for others.

There is so much hatred in this world and it does not need to affect you. The news is full of nothingness, rarely inspiring. Shut it off when it bothers you. I am not saying shut yourself off from the world; do not get caught up in the media mainstream. Bad stuff sells ads and picks up viewers. Do not be this person.

I am an animal Facebook freak. I love **"Dodo"** and other formats about animals. Some make me laugh, some make me cry. The ones that make me cry touch my heart in a warm way.

If you cannot find something that can warm your spirit, go to the library. Find a book on inspiration. Go to a shelter and help through services.

If you want to feel really good, stop reading after this paragraph, go to a gas station, or a grocery store, and give some money to someone in need. Leave no reason, just a smile, and walk away. The feeling of appreciation comes two-fold. From you and the recipient.

When we see people with less than us, we begin to appreciate the things in our lives we took for granted.

> *Good deeds create stronger light.*

I remember one time; I stopped at a gas station to buy a lottery ticket for a huge jackpot.

The person at the counter in front of me was digging change out of his pockets. He could not put together one dollar. The person behind the counter and one in front of me in line were chuckling.

By the time I got to the counter, I was upset and disappointed. I took all my money, which was not much, and said, "Put this in his tank. I am going to let him know to keep pumping ". When I told the man at the pump, he told me different excuses why he had no money. I could only say. **"It does not matter why; I wanted to do this to make sure you got to your next stop".** He smiled, thanked me and I smiled, turned, and walked away, telling him to have a great night.

I went back to the store and realized I had given this person all my money. Therefore, I did not play the lottery that night, but I did win big. I won the feeling of appreciation.

> *Hatred paralyzes life; love releases it. Hatred confuses life; love harmonizes it. Hatred darkens life; love illuminates it.*
> **Martin Luther King Jr**

> *Appreciate what you have and had, and the world will present the most beautiful things you never thought possible.*

CHAPTER 4

VISION

Without vision, the people will perish.
Proverb

Sadly, most do not see and never realize their dreams.

When we think about vision, we immediately think about the strength of our sight-- 20/20. My eyes are fine, but I must use reading glasses. Nearsighted or farsighted, we all see better out of one eye than the other. These are the ways we see the world and how we learn to function.

There is another vision that comes from within. Unlike seeing with our eyes, vision comes within our minds. Envisioning what we yet have. This sight helps us see the world through our feelings and it helps us to build our dreams and make our goals a reality.

The old saying, **"Profess it and you will get it,"** is a true way of getting the things in life you want. Professing is seeing something you desire as if you have it now. You must be able to visualize having it in your hand, driving it, living in it, wearing it, being it.

When I was 16, my brother was in Amway. I was too young, it wasn't for me anyway, but I did go to their seminars. These seminars were created to build you up, so you would see yourself become as successful as the speakers with the seemingly huge amount of wealth. A lot of these people faked their success to build their success. A lot of MLM, multi-layered marketing companies use this method today.

They prey on the person who wants success and does not know how to get it. They trap these people, showing off nice cars, jewelry, and houses. They tell them stories of their success promising them a pipe dream that only comes true for a small amount of people. I know people who fell into these hypes only to become in debt giving up on their dreams.

For me, I found an avenue from one of these

companies to help me in a different way. My brother was listening to a tape called Profess it and get it, recorded by a successful couple in Amway. I couldn't understand anything about life as a rich person, let alone their ways of thinking. I just couldn't see myself having this type of life. I was poor and insecure.

I listened to this tape. I was so hooked on the **"profess it and get it"** idea, I borrowed this tape and throughout the next five years, I listened to this tape over and over. I listened to this tape over 2000 times. It was so embedded in my head, that I could, to this date run the tape in my head with the speaker's Oklahoma ascents.

The tape made me realize the magic of the now. **"The Secret"** focuses on what everyone thinks is as important as material things and money. It taught me to dream and the power of visualizing to get what I desired out of life.

In this tape, they talked about looking at the things you wanted. Going to a car lot that had the car you desired, go through it, drive it. Even though you couldn't own it at that time, you could dream of having it. Driving it brought the realization of your vision of owning it.

I remember going to many jewelry stores to look at Rolex watches. They didn't have the model I wanted but to try on the name brand gave me the sense I could attain this vision of owning one. I went to huge homes visiting while they were having open houses looking and visualizing myself having this. I posted images of these items on my wall dreaming of having these status items. I remember having my sister take photos of me in front of these houses, so I could visualize living here.

These visualizations helped me attain a lot of

things in life. They also taught me I could accomplish anything I put my mind to. I had a friend who wanted to start his own church. He had no way of making this happen. He was a deacon at a local church and felt they weren't sharing the word of God properly and he wanted to create this. I reluctantly gave him the book, Think and Grow Rich and my valuable tape. This was the most valuable item I had ever owned as it taught me so many things about attaining things through visualization. I felt he needed it more than I did.

I appreciated learning from this one tape and what it did for me. 30 years later I located the couple who were on the tape to let them know my story. It took me over ten years to find them. Through the magic of the internet, I found them in Oklahoma.

When I talked to them, they were floored. How one tape could do so much for a person? The true purpose of this tape was meant to help find more dealers and build their downline of new sellers or people who dreamt of creating financial freedom.

They are still very successful people, in a new MLM company continuing to build other's dreams. I was asked to join their new organization and even though I wanted to become friends, that life was not for me, and I wasn't into living someone else's dream. We are now distant friends. I will always be grateful for what I was taught from that one cassette tape. I wish I still had it.

I did reach out to the minister of two churches. His dream came to reality. I am not sure if it came from the tape I used, but I know his vision was set when he decided to create his own path to his success.

I hope he still had this cassette tape and

unfortunately, he didn't. To this day, I search the internet to locate a copy. I will find it as I visualize myself having it again.

SETTING YOUR VISION

I had always wanted to own my very own restaurant. Using the visualization of what I learned, I wrote down my restaurant name and the description of service, I had my menu laid out with descriptions of each item. I carried this in a leather notebook and carried it with me all the time in my suitcase. I was a Corporate Chef for a company. Every time I did catering or set up an events menu, I would incorporate some of my ideas, honing my recipes. I was working on my dream, always keeping the visualization of having this place open.

For eight years, I kept this vision of opening my restaurant. One day, my wife and I were looking at some restaurant equipment from a closed restaurant that I intended to purchase and resell for profit. My wife said, "Gil, wouldn't this be a great place for that place you always wanted?" It was perfect! I couldn't believe my dream was coming to life. All these years of visualization paid off. It came to life. This whole time, I was living it without having it come to life.

I have built and sold numerous multi-million-dollar businesses and this one was it. My vision came to reality. I believe this one took so much time as I ventured into so many things at the time. The vision was there but at the time it was under the surface.

My point is this: I carried that idea around all those years, working on it. If I had stuck to that one vision, I would have obtained it much earlier in life.

Today, I know that if I don't attain something, it is either because I do not truly want it or because I do not see myself having it.

A MAN WITH GREAT VISION

In the eighties, I had the honor of working with the Great Mohamed Ali. He and his wife were in town promoting a fragrance called **"Ali'.** That week I spent with them was very educational for me as I had the honor of meeting a person who had the power of visualization. Ali at a very young age, knew he would be the greatest champion boxing ever had. He saw this at the age of seven years old. He knew when he started boxing, he was training to be the champ. He saw himself with the belt. His vision and belief were so strong. He fought for everything he believed in.

Ali gave up two of his prime years as a champion for his sight and beliefs in what was true to him. I remember his story and what I learned from him. He fought for civil rights and the belief that even though his title was pulled from him for those years, he still saw himself as the champ. After being reinstated and allowed to box again, Ali brought his vision back to reality and quickly became the undisputed champ. He is not only the best champion ever, he has left a legacy that very few humans have done in history that will live on forever.

THE SECRET TO BUILD YOUR SIGHT

I do an exercise with my clients where I ask them where

they see themselves in 5 years. Then we play a game where we act like are meeting for the first time, five years in the future.
I ask them the following:
- How are you doing?
- Man, I haven't seen you in… five years?
- So, what have you been up to?

The first couple of answers are easy for the person. The third is usually not answered correctly as we are used to seeing our experiences in the now and not able to see in the future.

Most people cannot talk as if the future is at this moment because they don't see themselves truly having the things they desire. You must be able to speak it as it is now at any moment. Without this strength, you will not possess the things in life you want.

We reverse roles, to enable them to realize they need to see themselves in that moment where they live and talk fluently about being five years into the future.

Without seeing yourself in the future, it is impossible to be able to have the things you want or be the person you want to be in life.

This is a great practice for you and others to play as it helps you develop your true sight for what you want in life. We need to see ourselves as it was five years from now living our dreams and having the things we want.

Jim Carey started with In Living Color. He decided to use this technique. He wrote himself a check for ten million dollars to be cashed on a certain date for services rendered in acting.

Jim carried this check with him all the time,

having to re-write the check as it fell apart in his wallet, copying every word.

Just shy of this date he set, he was paid ten million dollars for the lead role in **"Dumb and Dumber."** What made this come to life was the secret. The secret of seeing the outcome or goal set, the date, and the service he gave for the outcome.

These three steps must always be written. Ideally, you want to review it as much as you can and subliminally, you will see and read it just by seeing it folded in your wallet.

The book, or movie, The Secret tells you these steps and they make many believe this is all it takes. It is a multi-million-dollar business feeding off the weak. That is where they fool you. It is imperative that you do this like goals. (By the way, this is a super goal).

You must put action in it, see it already happening, and live every part of your life working hard at it. I always say, **"Work harder on yourself than you do at your job"**.

> *Desire is the burning to have something. Sight is being able to see, live, and have it.*

> *See more, have more.*

THE SIGHT OF DISNEY

There is a story about Walt Disney. He passed before Disney World was finished. Two of his top executives were standing on a hill, staring amazed at the finished Disney World.

One turned to the other and said, **"Man, isn't this something? Isn't it great? It would have been wonderful if Walt was here to see this."**

The other turned to him and said, **"He did see this, He did."**

Disney had it down. He could see it all. It was easy for him to create characters and describe them and the action they were going to take in storyboards and in his writing, and the artist could bring to life amazing movies in the form of cartoons. He also saw his Disney World before it was drawn up and built.

A VISION OF VIRGIN

Another one of my heroes, which I have talked about earlier in this book, is Sir Richard Branson.

Sir Branson's vision of what can become has made him and many others successful in life. From him seeing himself getting off the island he was stuck on due to a storm to realizing his actions could be a great business venture and started Virgin Airlines the many other business divisions in the Virgin world.

Sir Richard now sees a better world and is creating ways to help with our environment and energy issues. These things are being created now and will be realized after his death.

His vision is like no one else's. He sees the good in almost everything and can bring out the good in others.

Sir Richard had a vision of creating a ship that would take regular people into orbit for the experience and to improve travel. Everyone thought he was nuts. The most important person believed in him-- Himself.

He saw this ship, felt the G-Force as it took off, and could see it full of people, flying out of our orbit and returning to Earth, landing perfectly. He could see every curve of the ship, the shape of the wings, the seating, the color, and the cockpit where the captain flew the ship.

He knew when it would take its first fight and the service it would offer to normal people and the world.

I remember watching Sir Richard viewing Virgin Galactic as it was first flown. I saw and felt as if I was standing next to him and having the feeling Sir Richard had as the ship took off, went into orbit, and returned to Earth successfully.

The way he stood, and was breathing, could only be the most amazing feeling in the world. He was completing a vision that everyone said doubted. Here it was a beautiful, impossible bird created by many, from one person's sight.

> *We see with our minds, not our eyes.*

A great musician friend of mine, Tyler Williams, has Cerebral Palsy and is blind. Cerebral Palsy is a group of neurological disorders that appear in early childhood and permanently affect body movement and muscle coordination, disrupting the brain's ability to control movement and maintain posture and balance.

Tyler is an amazing musician. With this disorder, he still found a way to become an amazing guitar player and singer. The first time I heard him play the guitar, I was floored. You wouldn't know he had any issues with the beautiful sounds he creates.

When talking to Tyler, he talks as if he has sight. Tyler is completely blind but sees better than most. He doesn't see himself with any handicap issues but sees himself in a better world. I am so inspired when I talk to him. His words astound me. I wish I had the sight he possesses. He creates things we simply do not see in our minds.

It is amazing how our other senses take over and our brain causes us to increase the sensitivity of our other senses. With sight, we can see better when we improve our minds and the way we think.

I remember my sight was so bad because of the things that were going into my mind, not much positive sight of the world around or in me.

I could walk by a flower store and not even see the beauty of the vibrant colors. Today, I get floored as I catch a glimpse of a tiny flower or object that rattles my brain in appreciation for the sight of beauty.

> *Life is so much more amazing when we truly see the world.*

CHAPTER 5

SELF CONFIDENCE

I know I am better than I was told.

Earlier in this book, I talked about my upbringing and being part of a cult.

I told cruel things: **"You are evil, and you are going to burn them in a lake of fire while we all go to the promised land."** My parents used to put me in a closet at night with no lights, tell me this, and while I was in this pitch-black closet, I could hear them walk out of the house and slam the door shut.

I was six years old, and this was some scary shit! I had such a hard time dealing with my upbringing and abuse. I lived a life of fear and no self-worth.

Throughout my younger school years, I did well, academically. However, when it came time to be in front of the class for spelling bees, I froze up. I knew how to spell the words but could not get them outright. I would mix my words as if I were reading with my dyslexia.

As I got older, I remember the more excited or upset I got, the harder it was for me to function. My nerves were shot, and I shook like a Chihuahua. I would stutter so bad, it was horrifying.

I remember trying to interview for a job when I was 16. I was so nervous; I started shaking and almost hyperventilated. The manager got me a soda and said he would give me a moment to get myself in order.

I finally calmed down enough. He liked me and actually hired me. I think he felt sorry for me.

I was a great worker, just messed up inside. I was so scared; I never started that job. I couldn't do it; I was that scared.

Changes in life force us to build confidence.

I was fired from a job I loved once. I was so devastated and had to find a job that would pay me as well as I had before. I had my dream job. I was making a ton of money and ran the kitchens for numerous restaurants. This was a place where I was comfortable and could be the person I wanted to be, confident and cocky on the outside.

One day, the son of the owner came to the location and fired me on the spot. It was horrible. I saw myself working there forever. It was my safety zone for my poor self-esteem.

I found a job posting for an assistant manager at a large chain restaurant.

Again, while I was interviewing, I choked up. I knew one restaurant's system of operations and in no way was I qualified to be a manager for this company. I stuttered through the interview. I just could not answer any questions, except my name. I think I got that one right. I remember now.

Easy questions: I would freeze up for what seemed like hours. Tried to answer the questions, or just broke down and said, **"I just don't know."**

Needless to say, I was passed up for this position. By this time, I studied the restaurant and at the time, they had the best management-training program available and that was what I needed.

I called the interviewer and begged for a second chance. We scheduled another interview.

This time I was ready. I went to the library and studied tapes and books on building a better self-image, and interviewing techniques. Anything that would get me hired.

The interview day came, and the low self-esteem was back again, but I did well enough to be hired. The person who hired me said, "I am hiring you for one reason. Anyone who went through what you did to Making this second interview happen has to be special. I may be wrong, but I have this feeling about you."

I was hired! I was so excited. I was going to be the best! I would make him and myself proud.

Well, I started working and things I never thought I would have to do. Like directing older people, talking to customers, handling money, and talking to bosses in the corporate world. I was not in my comfort zone, that is for sure.

I was so bad, that my managing trainer pulled me into the storeroom, hiked his leg on a box, and said, "I know the person who hired you and he only hires good people. I just do not see it in you. Nevertheless, he knows what he is doing. Maybe there is something there, or maybe he finally made a bad choice."

I was devastated and scared. I thought I would be fired again. I could not let that happen. I was so scared of people older than I was, most likely due to my upbringing. I knew I had to fight or accept failure.

The next day, the manager who hired me stopped in and we had that talk everyone dreads. He had one more idea that might help and that would be my last chance. If this did not work, they invested in me, and both would lose.

I enrolled in Dale Carnegie's Communication and Human Relations course.

This course was amazing. It brought me out of my shell and created a new person. My awakening was so great; I became that dream manager I said I would be. I was performing the best in my position for a chain that had 260 restaurants. I turned three stores around bringing one from the bottom of the chain in performance to the top spot. Back then, bonus plans were amazing, and I made bank!

After three years with this company, I was off to my next vision of being a gourmet chef. I dropped my salary to one-third of what I was making to become a chef at a fine dining-restaurant.

The day I started my new vision of being a chef, I saw myself as the chef for this restaurant. The chef was cocky and knew it all. Or so he thought. I was that kid again on the stage becoming a Boy Scout with the vision of becoming an Eagle Scout in record time. I confidently decided then I would be the chef here within six months, and within four months, I studied and pushed so hard, I made it happen.

Throughout my career, I have created many successful operations, developed hundreds of people, and lived the life I always dreamed of.

This story was a small part of my success in life, but I wanted to share how becoming. whatever you want can happen if you just work on your confidence and build a healthier self-image.

Today, my focus is to inspire others to perform their best with the hope that I leave a part of myself instilled in their hearts.

It has been an honor seeing people grow from one person who started as a dishwasher and introvert, to high paying chef and leader for a large organization.

> *If you want a successful life, you must build your confidence and increase the value of who you are. Not what others see but what you see. Others will automatically see your greatness.*

AFFIRMATIONS TO BUILD YOUR STRENGTH

During my younger years, I found love in the weirdest places. My friends all in various gangs loved me because I was fearless when I was around them. I was young and searching for a home that never gave me love and family bonds. I found this in gangs. These people were my family, well I thought. One day during a scuffle, I saw these friends watch me as I took care of a situation they started. I turned during a scuffle and saw my friends standing there with these people they caused the issues with, just watching me. I realized then I wasn't part of them. I got up, left the situation and walked home 12 miles. That time allowed me to think of the path I was on. That evening, I was done. I was so done, and so lost.

While in school that year, I continued my bad behavior as this was what I thought continued my popularity with others. I was horrible on the outside. I continued to create havoc at school with others as I still thought this was who I was. I was in deep and inside I wanted to be done with it but couldn't figure it out.

I got into trouble in a class and was sent to detention. During my detention, the teacher who was there got tired of my terrible behavior and sent me to the principal's office. Before I left the class, he stopped me and said, "I don't know who you think you are, but this person you are portraying is not you. I see a much better person."

I was so upset. How could he say that? He did not know me. I walked home that day crying, cussing, yelling, **"Who does he think he is?"**

Those words he said sewed a seed in my soul. Every time I started to do something bad, I thought what he said. Then started saying, "I am a good person, and I am better than this. I am a damn good person." This was my first magical affirmation.

Let me tell you when someone is trying to belittle you and you yell out, "How dare you, you don't know me, I am a damn good person! You have no right to say this to me." It scares the hell out of people. They believe this. It scared the hell out of me as this affirmation started working on me. The more I said it, the more I believed it, the more it came to reality.

Those words from the detention teacher, Mr. Ronald Van Dresen opened my eyes to the person that was inside me all this time.

I didn't change overnight and as I said this in my head, what am I doing, I am a good person, I am better than this eventually stuck. Year after year, I used this affirmation to overcome my insecurities.

I wanted to say that later in my life, I finally reached out to Mr. Van Dresen. I told him the story and how he started this affirmation in me from his words. His words saved me, well, my life. He was floored, speechless after I told him my story. He said he needed a moment to take this all in. It isn't every day that someone in my situation does this. We met and had an amazing conversation, and

I was blessed that I had a chance to thank him in person for opening my heart and eyes. His words awoke the true person I was.

Ronald Van Dresen and I are meeting for dinner.

Sometimes we find ourselves vulnerable and that is the best time to bring out those affirmations. I do it when I need to. Lately, not much, as I deal with life in a completely different way that will be in my next book.

I teach this affirmation to others to help them build their strength from the insecurities they have. I had taken the legacy that Ronald gave me and passed it on.

So, what are affirmations? They are powerful

words we create. We read these aloud, repeating them over and over to make us stronger internally and help us create the things we want in life.

When creating your affirmations, they must be something that you may not see yourself achieving now but knowing if you read them daily you can create these stretched affirmations.

> *We do not know what we are capable of creating for ourselves, so nothing is truly out of reach or non-achievable.*

Remember there are people out there that will tell you to do affirmations every day and it will come to life. Well, they will, providing you build your knowledge and work harder on yourself than you do at your job.

Perform at your best on the job, but work harder on yourself. Study and learn as much as you can. Stretch yourself. Believe you can accomplish anything.

Nothing comes easy. Do not fall for the hype sold by the systems like "The Secret." They are selling you on a pipe dream. They never tell you how much work you need to put in to attain these secrets. The true secrets are the titles in this book and live a life surrounded by the things that make you happy. If you want wealth, find something you love and create a service to the masses around that. Serving others is no secret.

Affirmation for some that use them to manifest things in life uses the future as it is now. Like the chapter on vision. Here are some samples of affirmations you can use for health, wealth and happiness.

AFFIRMATIONS

DAILY AFFIRMATIONS FOR WEALTH

- Money is an unlimited resource, and it is always flowing my way.
- I allow my $ ___________ months to come quickly and easily. They are so easy, I let them be easy.
- Every single day, more and more money keeps flowing into my life.
- I get highly paid for being me.
- I am so grateful that people love to pay me.
- My bank account is growing at a rapid speed.
- It is safe for me to be a wildly wealthy man/woman.
- There is always more where that came from.
- I am a money magnet. I love money and it loves me.
- I attract money in the most incredible expected and unexpected ways.
- I am open and ready to receive my unlimited divine wealth right now.

VACATION PLANS:

- Dear universe, I am open and ready to receive the exact funds that I need to be on this trip. _________________ I am so grateful that I have booked my trip to _________________ this _____________________________ for fun in the sun. Thank you, thank you, thank you!

- The money that I needed to go to __________________ came so quickly and so easily.

HEALTH

- Weighting __________ pounds feels so good I move faster light on my feet.
- I love the accolades I get from people seeing me this healthy.
- Every single day, my health improves. My breathing is so strong.
- This size ____________ cloths looks so great on me. It is phenomenal to buy cloths from a normal store. No more specialty shops and clothes that don't fit.
- I am young again! I feel fifteen years younger!

> *Someone is sitting in the shade today because someone planted a tree a long time ago.*
> **Warren Buffett**

CHAPTER 6

KNOWLEDGE

Work harder on yourself than you do at your job.
Jim Rohn

Sadly, most do not and never realize their dreams.

> *We must have specialized knowledge to accomplish what we want.*

We don't have to be the best in our field or our services, we have to understand our specialty, know our competition, and understand what our knowledge can do for us.

Your idea of your super goal may already have been created or out in the market. Maybe your product is a little better than theirs.

When we desire to have or get something in life, we have to look at knowledge as a huge part of attaining the things we want.

As a child, I knew there was better out there for me. I knew I was better than what I was told. I set out to prove this and realized, in order to grow, I needed to improve my skill set. At the age of eight, while in school, I worked in the cafeteria washing pots and pans. They wouldn't let me work on the line or take lunch tickets because I was a poor and dirty kid.

I enjoyed this work as it had a reward, all the pizza I could eat! I ate about 12 pieces or more. Burnt, I did not care it was food I would not have at home and it was yummy.

WE ARE THE SUM OF OUR THOUGHTS

We become what we think about all day long. I learned the more efficient I got the more they liked me. This was my first idea of building my skill set. I was increasing my knowledge on how to become a better pot washer and cleaner, so as I got better, so did the meals and the love from the cafeteria ladies.

My passion for food started here. I knew I would be in this field forever and someday own one of those fancy restaurants. Now back then Frisch's Big Boy was fancy to me. My first job was in a Mexican restaurant as a busboy. I learned everything about this and how to become better, so I could be the best. Then moving to a dishwasher position, quickly moving to cook then to Kitchen Manager manager. I was great, well not as a leader, a great worker.

I was building my skills, but not my mind. I didn't realize this was needed to improve my self-esteem, and my leadership knowledge to get others to perform better. My mind thought. "If I am the best working rings around everyone, I am in and so valuable, they couldn't survive without me.

Well, this turned into cockiness, and lack of appreciation for the owner's son who got upset with me, as I wouldn't listen to his direction and he fired me.

What a wake-up call. I realized I was out on the streets again with no job and no money coming in. I was so upset; I couldn't believe he could do this.

Searching and being interviewed for a job was tough and being rejected made me realize I had to learn how to be stronger person and learn how to communicate better with people to get the job I wanted.

Once I got the job and started turning myself around, I used education from books, small business, and leadership classes to improve myself as a leader. I became a better leader performing at the top, and this time learning the smart way.

I took everything, every course I could afford to take. If work wouldn't pay for it, I did. I was on fire.

"Work harder on yourself than you do at your job", is one of my favorite quotes from Jim Rohn. I have committed myself to this quote all my life and when you have dyslexia, you really must work on it.

Education for me was the thing that brought me out of my poor self-image, it has put me at the top of my performance in everything I do. Every day, I study to improve who I am, so I can continually help others get what they want. Everything I the study is focused on reaching my full potential in serving others. Books, audio, magazines, the internet, and even movies. If there isn't a leadership of life learning message in a movie, I cannot watch it.

Sounds boring to some I am sure, but to me, I feel better knowing it is making me a better person.

Writing this book took a lot of work for me as I wasn't a good reader and when I wrote, it was like a puzzle. The first time I wrote an article on leadership. I had my wife and my daughter proofread it. They couldn't make sense of what I was writing. I had to rewrite it twice and re-organize it. I wrote as I read.

In the fourth grade, I was put in a special reading group. This was devastating to me as I felt stupid. I was smart, but the teacher put me back because of reading. I was great with words and understanding them but put them in a paragraph and I was lost. Dyslexia was not my friend.

I never told many people about my reading issue and later in life, I fought through it. When I have a project, I don't wait, I move on it quickly being the first usually to be completed so I can restructure my words to make sense to others.

Today I have many articles published in numerous magazines and sights on leadership and inspiration in life situations. This is my second book, and it has been so inspiring to me knowing just a few years ago, I couldn't write an article together without help.

Now when I write, it still at times can be a jumbled puzzle, but after I read it, I can now complete my puzzle, so people can understand my work. I am proud of this since reading and writing were my worst areas of learning.

Is this book perfectly written? No, but it is a major accomplishment for me as I see where my thirst for education and knowledge has taken me. I am sure my next book will be even better.

When I was the fourth grader, that was moved back, I could have accepted that I was not good at English and writing, but I didn't. Even though it broke my spirit a bit, I pushed myself and continue, to this day, working harder on myself than I do at my work. Everyday. There are days when I feel I didn't do enough and when I look back on my day, I accomplished a lot.

When we are faced with adversity, we can either give up and accept it or become better at who we are to overcome it.

The best way to win in life and build a healthier self-image is to build your knowledge. Start and never think you know it all. There is always something new and exciting to learn.

THE MIRROR TELLS THE TRUTH

About four years ago, a dear friend of mine who is strong in the study of spirituality taught me about using a mirror to see who we are. He had me one day look in a mirror and say, "I love you." I thought this was the stupidest thing I have ever done. I laughed; I couldn't say it.

That evening, I went home and tried it. I came to the reality that I wasn't loving or comfortable with the person in the mirror. I had to dig deep down to understand why. I meditated and reflected on this process and realized I wasn't comfortable because I wasn't true to myself.

I practiced every day and worked on the things I didn't like seeing in the mirror. As time went on, I looked and smiled and loved the person. Although I am not perfect, I appreciate who I am and who I have become. I see a different person looking back at me. One who is appreciative of who I am and what I do. I realized that I became a much more in-tuned person for who I am and what I reflect to others. I see what they see.

Looking in the mirror saying I love you is not conceited; it is looking into your soul realizing you are a great spirit and you have a lot to give to the world. Sometimes we do not like what we see, because we are becoming true to ourselves. We can change this view by changing what goes into our minds. Once we love ourselves then, and only then, can we share this love or light we burn to others.

There is an old story about the emperor with no clothes. He was a conceded person only out for himself. No one was as good as him. No one would tell him.

One day he wanted to show the world that quietly hated him how great he was. He ordered the best tailor in the land to design an emperor's outfit like no one had ever seen. The designer decided that it would be fitting for this emperor to show the people whom he treated so badly what he was about.

He met with him and showed him the finest silk thread. It was so fine; you couldn't see it. The emperor, knowing he was smarter and better than everyone else was, thought I don't see it, yet it must be there. Therefore, he said; "It is perfect! Make me the best design you have ever created. It must be the greatest in all the land. The tailor went to his shop and worked on the outfit. Later he went back to have the emperor fit the cloths.

The emperor's servants were in on what was happening. He tried it on, looked in the mirror, and saw no clothes but everyone was astounded by the beauty of the clothes. So, he said this is amazing. Take it back, tailor it and I shall wear this to the parade to show it off.

The day came, and he put on the clothing including from the robe created of the same fine silk. Everyone again was amazed at how stunning this outfit was. The emperor didn't see it in the mirror however he was the smartest and thought, "If they see it, I am greater and smarter than all of them so I, of course, do also.

That day during the festivities, the emperor strutted down the streets showing off his new clothes. Designed and sewn together with the finest of silk. Everyone cheered as he pranced down the streets.

He came to a boy who said to his mother. **"Look he has no clothes, he is naked"**. The crowd murmured then started laughing at him. The emperor realized he was fooled into seeing what wasn't there and ran off in shame. You see the emperor saw who he truly was in the mirror the whole time, but because of him not being true to himself, he became blind to what was real.

> *Look into the mirror and see who you are. If you don't love what you see, change it.*

CHAPTER 7

DECISION

Decide and stick to it.

DECISIONS IN LEADERSHIP AND BUSINESS

The greatest leaders are the ones who make decisions and stick to them. No one can sway them. They are confident in their choices.

It was said that Henry Ford was one of the most decisive people of his time.

When he decided to create the Model T and its production assembly line, Ford put a plan together and moved on with his decision. The assembly line was a huge success and is used in so many companies today.

As other car dealers developed their cars, Henry never swayed from the design. It worked. Yet all the other car manufacturers were creating fancy-looking cars. Henry's leadership team tried to convince him to change the look of the Model T as it was outdated and becoming unpopular. It took a long time for Henry to agree to change the model and then it took even longer for this change to happen. The idea was someone else's, and because of this, it took a lot to convince Henry Ford to change.

DECISIONS IN OUR PERSONAL LIVES

In our personal lives, we have things we want to accomplish. Though we want to realize these successes, we fail to accomplish them as we change our minds about how important these decisions are for us.

We start working on a goal and at first, we have this drive to create our vision. Then life takes over. We have things that get in the way, we find it hard to move forward and then we realize the progress is so slow, that we dump our dreams. This is common and most don't realize that success could have been through the next step they took. I do it, we all do it.

What we do not realize is every time we change our minds, it weakens our ability to make sound choices in the things that should be important to us. We go through life not understanding why we cannot get ahead or attract good things like others.

STICK TO YOUR PLAN

I once knew a person who was great at anything they chose to do. They were naturally talented in art, running a business, and developing others. The sad thing is, they never stuck to their guns on things that were important to them. This person would decide on a project, and halfway through, they would start questioning what should be done. They couldn't see the finished product or the achievement of its success once the project was completed.

Never happy with their performance and jobs, this person would tell me, **"I decided to look for another position, this one is going nowhere."**

For two years, I heard them announce this. Today, they are still employed by the same company, saying the same thing, and still completely miserable. Why is it that is so hard to make and stick to a decision?

When we continually change our minds on the things we want to accomplish, we never get anything done.

I remember as a young manager; I was afraid to make decisions. I was easily manipulated into thinking my ideas wouldn't work and it would chip away at my self-esteem. Needless to say, I failed miserably as a manager. I was fired from my first management position. In my mind, it was everyone's fault, but my own.

Being a successful leader includes traits that are learned when one is younger. I grew up in a very unstable household.

As a teenager, I went from friend's house to friend's house for a place to live or searched for family within my school district. Armed with persuasive skills and excuses, I somehow always found a place to stay. Sometimes it was only for a night, sometimes a week or even a month until the families got tired of me and kicked me out. It was difficult with no stability, so I was forced to quit school.

Not having a permanent home kept me from believing I could find a home and finish school. Constantly moving around became an excuse for my poor decision-making. I taught myself nothing was permanent through the uncertainties of my homelessness.

The first time in my life that I actually found the beginning of a permanent home, was when I met my first wife. I knew her from work and dated her once and moved in on the second date. I am not sure if she realized this, but I needed a change in my life and had decided this was going to be my permanent home.

She lived in a huge home that was her parents. They had both passed years prior. My hope in life was to have a nice home, a family, and a good job. Marrying her gave me all three of these. This was wrong on my part.

I realized a couple of years after we were married, that my life still didn't change. I was still insecure and couldn't make my mind up as to what I wanted.

I finally came to the realization that I messed her life up by pushing her to move in and to marry me. I was a jerk. To this day, I am not sure if I ever told her that. I do believe she saw this.

I finally made the decision to leave the marriage. We weren't happy. This weird way of making a decision and sticking to it. It was the right decision and a good start for my decisive moves, but it was only the beginning of my education.

> *Decide and move on it.*

During my first job as a manager, I was lacking in leadership skills, and I decided it would be best for me to go back to school. I was making very good money back then, enough to be able to buy my mother a home at a very young age.

Something was missing in my life, and I realized it was the thought that I quit school without really giving it a hard chance. I decided that year to put every part of my free time into studying. Here I was a miss-driven person, finally making a decision to study my head off to get a GED. It was then that I learned I had dyslexia. It was scary to know I would have to work twice as hard to comprehend the work that was needed and to succeed.

Because I was doing well financially, and my friends did not understand what success really meant, they would ask me why I went back to school. I would hear time and time again, **"You are wasting your time.**

You make great money, and you have a great job and future." It was a simple idea that if I didn't finish school, I would have wasted ten years of my life. (I quit school in the tenth grade).

Every day, I would get off work, go to the park, and study. I re-read everything to understand my schoolwork. At times, I would go to the library for videos that could better explain what I was reading. Night school was especially helpful. I realized that if I could have stayed in high school and applied myself, I could have made it happen.

I stuck to my vision of finishing school. I never listened to the nay-sayers or questioned my decision. My focus was to not waste those ten years of school I had already pushed through. It wasn't easy. I didn't have any support, but I still got through it on my own.

> *Once you decide on something, don't let you or anyone change your mind.*
> *It is your future, your dreams and desires, and does not affect them.*

If it weren't for that one cassette I listened to over 2000 times, that taught me to profess things and I would get them, I don't think I would have stayed the course. As a matter of fact, I don't believe I would have even gone back to school.

Like so many of my friends and family, I wouldn't have understood the desire to dream big. This "waste of ten years of my life," was instilled in my brain. I could see myself getting that dream job once I had this diploma in my hand. No one was going to change my mind. Yes, I was making great money, even by today's standards. But I needed to finish school. I was committed to this decision.

This commitment sewed the seed to realize that once we make a decision stick to it. Don't listen to anyone's doubt, especially in your mind. It will play tricks on you as the fear creeps up. You will make mistakes; however, we learn from them. Never quit and move in a different direction, stay focused on your outcome.

I once worked for a company where the founder was a truly decisive person. He and his brother started a vending company, and it grew into an impressive business. It started with vending cigarettes, snack machines, and then food service operations in corporate offices and factories.

He was a person who knew what he wanted, made a decision, and you were not going to change that no matter what. Every move was made with confidence and because of his confidence, he was quite intimidating to everyone.

Everyone was scared of this man. When he made a decision, right or wrong, no one argued with him.

This was great for him. When he decided to expand to café or cafeteria services, he did not know this type of food service well and needed to change the direction of the company for continual growth. The decisions up to that point were spot on.

Since he didn't understand how the food industry changed in taste, his services became out of date.

He hired a person to change the way they did food service. This person was a mentor of mine and was a visionary for this type of service. I was brought on as a corporate chef to upgrade the food and implement new services to meet the new demands of the company's growing clientele and food standards.

A plan of change was put in place, and the owner fought with the change. He couldn't relinquish the control of business to someone else. Even though he knew it could improve his sales and profits.

After months of meetings and fights with him, he finally accepted the change and actually stepped to the side and let his son run the company.

A year later he retired and controlled his son's decisions behind the scenes. Sadly, he passed, and his son now had the company's future in his hands.

The son was nothing like his father. The father had a cold snarl on his face and knew what he wanted. The son smiled and had the highest integrity, but low self-esteem.

Because of his low self-image, he could not make a decision. One moment he would make one, the next, someone would comment about it, and he would quickly change his mind.

The company eventually lost money and was forced to sell. The inability to make a decision created failure.

> *Listening to others may be good or bad.*

There are so many people in our lives who seem to believe they know what is good for us. They criticize our thoughts, our actions, and if you look at their lives, they are no better off than we are.

Why do they think they know what is good for us when they don't have their lives in order? When you set a plan, decide on what you want, and people will intervene, and they will. So just smile, thank them and **STICK TO YOUR DECISION!**

It's all about you, your happiness, and life, not others. If they were wrong, it doesn't affect them, it only affects you.

You have to make your mind up on what you want and stick to your plan. We all make mistakes and that is ok. The idea is to learn from them. If there are huge mistakes, get back up brush them off, and go again, set your target a little different until you are successful.

DECISIONS AND CHICKENS

There was a man in his 70's who loved chicken. He loved it so much that he developed what he believed was the best fried chicken recipe out there. He decided one day to go out and sell his chicken recipe. He packed his car, and, on the road, he went.

It seemed like every place he went to, closed the door in his face, and asked him why they needed his recipe when theirs was just as good. When he was able to get in the door of businesses, he did his cooking and they all said no.

Each time someone said no, he looked at how he was approaching them. He knew he had the best product out there and someone was going to buy it. He decided what he wanted, believed in it, and didn't give up.

Finally, after hundreds of times, someone loved his recipe and it started. Kentucky Fried Chicken was born.

Colonel Sanders was a very decisive man. He already knew the outcome of what he set out to do.

Confident, he pushed and pushed until he finally got the answer her was searching for.

YES.

Was his chicken better than most? Maybe, maybe not. The difference is his belief and commitment to his decision to sell this. KFC is a multi-billion-dollar company today. I personally don't care for the place as it isn't the colonel's original recipe anymore, but I do care for the desire he had to create his dream and bring it to life by one decision.

Oh, I did get to meet the Colonel when I was young. He scared me because he was the man on the bucket.

GET YOUR VIRGINITY

Years ago, there was a young man who loved to travel and party. One day, he was on an island with friends. While he was having fun, in his mind, he wanted to figure out what his life could become. This bothered him, although he was still young, he felt empty not knowing what his future would bring. The job he had was OK but not exciting, definitely not what he wanted to do all his life.

At the end of his trip, a storm was heading through the islands. Because of the threat of the storm, the airport canceled most of the flights.

In his determination to get home, he came up with an idea. Locate a plane and a pilot and offer him money to fly him home.

THE REVEAL

Finding the plane and pilot was easy, the hard thing was getting the money to pay for gas and the pilot. He had no money left from his trip.

He thought, "How I can charter a plane, get enough people to pay for the trip and get off the island." He simply wrote a sign: "Who wants to go home? Come fly with us." He was able to find enough people to not only to pay for the flight but put some money in his pocket.

His decision to want to go home and stick to this created the idea. This decision was so successful for him that he started his first company, Virgin Airlines. Yes, Sir Richard Branson started Virgin on a decision and desire.

Make a decision and decide that nothing will change this. The idea when you are committed will reveal itself. Who knows, you may be the next Richard Branson.

LET THERE BE LIGHT. THE STORY OF EDISON'S LIGHT BULB.

Edison, we all know, was an amazing inventor. His work included so many ideas. One of his biggest inventions was the incandescent light bulb.

Edison wanted to be the first person to illuminate the night with a product that wouldn't need the oil and other temporary accelerants. He tries many different filaments including string and different types of wires. Most would burn up immediately some wouldn't work at all. In all, it took ten thousand tries to get it right. When asked why he decided to try this and fail so many times Edison replied, **"I didn't fail ten thousand times, I**

just found ten thousand ways it wouldn't work."

Once he decided to create the first light bulb, he committed to his discussion.

To this day, I use Edison bulbs in my home. An oddly shaped bulb with an amber color that causes that yellowish effect. Although these bulbs aren't the brightest, I use them as inspiration for me to keep commitment to my decisions.

> *Decide on your life's plan. You can include others but not in the decision.*

We will realize our dreams when we realize the strength of making and sticking to them. So, decide today, what it is you want out of life.

CHAPTER 8

PERSISTENCE

Never take no for an answer.

Sadly, most do, never realizing their dreams.

I have talked about not taking "no' for an answer. Before I got my first leadership role, I was turned down for the position. I didn't take the no for an answer. I pushed myself and did whatever I needed to do in order to get the position I wanted. After persisting, I received the opportunity, and it changed my life.

When I was younger, I didn't have the confidence to realize I could have fought to become the Eagle Scout I worked so hard to be. Instead, I gave up and lost my desire.

So many of us accept rejections, and time after time we eventually never reach for what we want because of fear of failure and hearing **"No."**

When it comes to promotions, or asking for the money we want/deserve, we don't go after the job we feel we can do because of fear of rejection. We take new jobs and are hired for less than what we are worth. because we think it is all they will give. We settle.

> *You get what you ask for.*

I worked for a large manufacturing company as a corporate chef and general manager. One of our contracts needed upgrading to all of their food service operations. I met with our VP of sales and the president of our company. We discussed what was needed and the big part of the conversation was what they thought they would get. I asked, **"Why aren't we asking for what we need?"**

The VP of sails said **"We won't get it, so we aren't going to ask. There is no way they would go for it."** A billion-dollar company, who clearly had the funds and wanted to best for their employees, was willing to take a fraction of what was needed because of the fear of rejection.

At the meeting with the executive team of the company, they praised our services. Our VP started his talk about how we could increase our service. Then he did it, he asked for less than what we talked about. I interjected and said, "What he is asking for is what he thought you might agree to, and it isn't close to what is actually needed to make any difference."

The VP was not happy. The President of our company froze. I was on the hook. I told my story and the reasons, and the top person asked me what it would actually take. I discussed the equipment needed, and then the amount with the outcome of what we could do if they accepted the proposal.

They didn't agree to exactly what I presented; however, it was ten times the amount we were originally asking. Not only were we able to get the majority of what we wanted, we could increase our production and performance. I looked pretty good that day. I also got scolded for cutting in on this meeting and making the VP look bad, but the president of our company could breathe better knowing I was right.

If we had gone the other route, we would not have been able to improve on anything making us look even worse. To try to get out of that situation after someone invested what you asked for would have been embarrassing.

We must have value in ourselves and what we do and ask to be compensated for it accordingly. Demand it. We deserve it, you deserve it.

This was a turning point in my life. I understood

the value of what we do when we aren't afraid of rejection and stick to our values.

As children, we were always told no. **"No, don't do that."** In my case, I was told I was not good enough and I would never amount to anything.

I remember in the ninth grade; I took an aptitude test. When I met with the student counselor to review the results, the counselor told me that I would be good with my hands. I asked what this meant.

She said, **"You would be a great factory worker where you can work with your hands."** I was stunned. How could this person know this about me by one test? I could have believed them and went with this.

Even though my self-esteem was so low, I did not believe this. I knew I was better than that. I knew if I accepted this, I would have not been successful. There is nothing wrong with manual labor, it just wasn't my plan. I saw myself being better and doing amazing things with my life. I just didn't know how and all my friends and family were this type of person she was describing to me.

When Taylor Swift decided she was going to be a singer, she knew she was there, she saw she was it. Thousands of people go to Nashville to become that next country singer.

The reason why they fail, well one is they can not perform, the other is that the truly talented miss it because of their lack of persistence and lack of belief in themselves. Just because thousands of people don't make it, doesn't mean you can't. They go to Nashville knowing the possibility of failure. Swift went there knowing she was that star.

Don't take no for an answer. Swift didn't and look at her today. A net worth of $350,000.00,.00 and an annual salary of over $150,000,00.00. There are much better performers than her who tried, they just didn't see it like she did.

It is scary when you don't value yourself you question your worth to the world. You then find yourself going backward, wondering why things don't work out for you.

When I coach people, it is hard to make them understand their true value. I have to instill in them the realization that they are worth more than they think. Shoot high and you will receive what you deserve shoot low and you might get the job, but you will always have the 'what ifs". If we are miserable at our jobs, it is because we settled, and it is usually our fault. The rejection should come from you saying, **"Thank you, but I will pass."**

I get a lot of offers, but they aren't what I want or do not show the value of what I bring to the table. I know my worth. I know that I may not have all the knowledge to do the complete job, but that's fine as I have proven in the past my leadership skills and knowledge of what I do I can do. I can do anything put in front of me. My strengths overcome the skills I may not have at that time.

I am worth more and I know this. As it says in the title of this book, **"I know I am better than what I was told."** You are worth more. then you know. You are better than what you were told, no matter what it was. You have to believe it.

So, I am cool with no's, I am even better with, **"Are you kidding me? I wouldn't pay anyone that!"** You should be fine with, **"You don't have what it takes."** You do.

If the people at your place of employment do not see the value in you, keep on pushing, someone else will. It happens every day.

Work harder on yourself than you do at your job. Perform at your best while working, and always be working on improving your knowledge, and your skill level. Companies will invest in you; however, it isn't enough to get you to where you want to be in life to stand out in the world.

In three years, investing just one hour of your day towards bettering yourself can put you at the head of your field of work.

Within five years, you will become an authority in your field. In ten years, you will become one of the top in your field in the world.

A lot of my free time is spent studying to create a better me. I always inventory my life. I look at where I was six months ago, one year ago, five years ago, etc. If I don't see improvements, I ask, **"What can I do differently?"** or **"Am I doing enough?"**

We don't know completely what we are capable of until we try. When we take inventory, we see our accomplishments and the level of improvement. Be persistent in everything you do and never take no for an answer.

I worked with a large Japanese auto manufacturer in the 90's. One of their top executives taught me their beliefs in manufacturing and the pursuit of constantly improving their methods and quality, **"Kaizen"**. They learn of a product, and research. it, try to replicate it but improve it just a little bit. Then daily, work towards making a tiny improvement every day.

This tiny improvement every day becomes a huge accomplishment. This is why they have done so well as a leading country.

Every day, we need to spend the necessary time honing our skills to get to where we want to be. The sad thing is, we try too hard the first few days and quit because it is too hard.

Health is a great example. We decide we want to become healthier. We join a gym, start working out, and after a couple of hard workouts, we feel burning and pain in muscles we didn't know we had. We take a few days off to rest then never return. The only thing that continues in the gym is the monthly payments.

Start off a little slower and work your way up.

> *Some hit the gym hard and continue, most don't. Some hit life hard and keep pushing, but most don't.*

When we go for career advancement or change, we may not get the opportunity we are searching for at first. We need to continue our push to make it happen. Be persistent in all you do and want. It will eventually come.

Sometimes not getting one opportunity was just meant to be as there are always better opportunities just down the road.

CHAPTER 9

THE SECRET TO IMMEDIATE CONFIDENCE

Building your inner strength to immediately conquer anything.

> *We are the sum of our thoughts. We become what we think about all day long.*

There have been many times in my life I needed a tiny push of encouragement to get me through a tough situation. We all have had that issue where fear and doubt take over and we just can't seem to move toward what scares us.

Facing tough situations can be very difficult. Sadly, most people just skip it and live a life of playing it safe. These people never realize their true inner strength and what it can do for them.

There was a study done where 100 people over 80 years of age were asked the question, "If you had your life to live over what you might do differently?" The majority said they would take more chances in life. Wow! Take more chances. When do we realize how important this is to us? This is a secret of living a truly exceptional life, a life rarely lived.

Any successful people you read about or talk to, will tell you that taking a chance is the most powerful thing you could ever do.

They would tell you that with every failure they had, getting up again and taking another chance at their vision was the personal secret to their successful life.

> *No action brings no results.*

When I left home at the age of 13 to find out who I was; when I was turned down for that job I wanted, I couldn't take no for an answer; When I went after my GED with dyslexia and the fear of not being smart enough; When I started my first business with no money, but used my salesmanship and ingenuity; When I took hundreds of chances like these, I look back today and think, if I passed on one, just one, I would have been a failure today. I never would have found my purpose or realized my dreams.

I didn't always make the perfect decisions and I failed many times, but I never let this stop me. I fell hard, brushed it off, and kept going. Les Brown says it best, **"When you fall, land on your back. You can only look up!"**

Every day I stretch my comfort zone. I live by strong leadership skills and am one who breaks the rules without breaking the laws. What this means is, when someone says something cannot be done, prove them wrong and become the first one to do it!

I have never lived life between the lines. I actually colored this way, always going outside the lines. However, coloring was never my strong point.

If I messed up, I claimed it and accepted the consequences. If I didn't and someone used me as a scapegoat, watch out. I became the bear that protected the cubs. I protect my integrity, as I am the only one who can violate this.

There are times when I am not 100% sure of the approach to something so I have a true secret. This secret will get you through anything.

When we are afraid or have low self-esteem, we slouch, our breathing becomes increasing, we shake, and our **"eye of the tiger"**, becomes **"the butt of a kitten."** Nothing good comes from this mental state.

SUPERPOWERS!

Every one of us has this hidden power within us. Yes, even you!

Before you have something that is difficult for you, meeting someone for the first-time interviewing, getting in trouble, and a huge one, facing a spouse or person who wants to control you or make you feel inferior.

They are out there, and most people allow this abuse. There is a way to put you in a state that will put you in control.

If we don't have the strength awakened inside of us, it will not show on the outside.

I learned an exercise from a good friend, and it has been around for years.

I'm Superman or Superwomen!

Photo by Jennifer Evans and her Defiance College of Ohio team.

THE SUPERHERO POSE

So, it's out! We all have superpowers. This is true. In the Bible, it says, **"We were created in the image of God."** If this is true, we are all amazing spirits. We have the power of the unimaginable.

Our superpowers come out when we are in danger. There are many stories of accidents and small people in the heat of the moment, lifted huge objects to save someone.

The Super person's power comes from a simple idea.

Earlier, I talked about slouching and breathing. These are parts of our nervous system, and it changes our physiology.

When we are timid, our bodies react to our posture, breathing, and mindset. The mind and body do what our spirit dictates.

The easy fix is when our superhero is getting ready to fly and save the world, they always stand in the Super person pose; back straight, chest out, hands on their side, and head up, then they take off! Up, up, and away!

OK, one slight secret is missing. They cut the camera recording the superhero/actor standing in their pose. Then action! The superpowers have now kicked in and with editing, it seems as if they fly off and save the earth.

Now we know the second step doesn't happen. There are no cameras in our lives. So, in real life, just before you take on your fear.

Become your superhero. Stand in the super person pose; back straight, chest out, hands on your side, and head up. Do this and hold this pose for no less than two minutes. 120 seconds and not one second less!

Deep inside our body, our blood is rushing, breathing is strong and paced right, the stance we have is stern, our physiology is changing, and our spirit is awakening. Your mind and nervous system are racing, bringing oxygen to major parts of your body. The endorphins are having a party. Then it kicks in—your mind says to your inner person, "Oh shit, what is happening? We are invincible. Let us go kick some ass!" All the fear, uncertainty, and poor self-image just disappears. You are now ready for your flight and fight.

This helps in all areas of our lives: before a test, interviews, meeting the new in-laws, dealing with that terrible boss, the bully, and confronting the abusive person in your life by making a choice to move on with your life (please never place yourself in danger by resorting to physical violence). I want you to stick up for yourself and realize how superhuman you are, and how important you are to yourself and the world. To hell with this person who tries to control you. You are a super person! A high spirit.

Give this a try and spread it to others. I have taught this to so many people, and it has pushed them to the next level. There is nothing stronger than building a positive self-image. It works and has worked for me and everyone I've taught it to.

I promise you, this is it. Once you realize the power of our minds and the utilization of our physiology, you will awaken to a new person.

What we hold on to on the inside shows on the outside.
We must change our inner thoughts to brighten our light!

Thank you for reading my book.
Please contact me on my website at
www.gilevans.net

9 798330 238736